BOSTON HARBOR

1. Snake Island
2. Deer Island
3. Green Island
4. The Graves (Graves Light)
5. Little Calf Island
6. Calf Island
7. Outer Brewster Island
8. Middle Brewster Island
9. Shag Rocks
10. Little Brewster Island
    (Boston Light)
11. Great Brewster Island
12. Lovells Island
13. Nixes Mate
14. Gallops Island
15. Georges Island
16. Long Island
    (Long Island Head Light)

17. Spectacle Island
18. Thompson Island
19. Moon Island
20. Rainsford Island
21. Hangman Island
22. Peddocks Island
23. Nut Island
24. Raccoon Island
25. Sheep Island
26. Bumpkin Island
27. Grape Island
28. Slate Island
29. Worlds End
30. Langlee Island
31. Ragged Island
32. Sarah Island
33. Button Island
34. Webb State Park

n

Miles

0   1

ISBN-13: 978-1-889833-91-0
ISBN-10: 1-889833-91-6

Library of Congress Cataloging-in-Publication Data

Morss, Sherman.

 Boston Harbor Islands / photographs and text by Sherman Morss, Jr.

   p. cm. — (The New England landmarks series)

 ISBN 1-889833-91-6

 1. Boston Harbor Islands (Mass.)—Pictorial works. 2. Boston Harbor Islands (Mass.)—Description and travel. 3. Boston Harbor Islands (Mass.)—History. I. Title. II. New England landmarks.

 F73.63.M67 2005

 917.44′61—dc22   2004029164

Cover and interior design by Peter Blaiwas, Vern Associates, Inc.
Map on endpapers by Jeffery M. Walsh
Printed in Korea.

Commonwealth Editions
266 Cabot Street, Beverly, Massachusetts 01915
www.commonwealtheditions.com

The New England Landmarks Series

Cape Cod National Seashore, photographs by Andrew Borsari
Walden Pond, photographs by Bonnie McGrath
Revolutionary Sites of Greater Boston, photographs by Ulrike Welsch

Front cover: Boston Harbor and skyline from Outer Brewster Island
Back cover: Snowy egret, Sarah Island rookery

Boston Harbor Islands

PHOTOGRAPHS AND TEXT BY SHERMAN MORSS JR.

COMMONWEALTH EDITIONS
Beverly, Massachusetts

ost Boston residents and visitors know something about the city's inner harbor. It is plainly visible from the downtown waterfront and the North End, from the Charlestown Navy Yard, and from Logan International Airport. But relatively few are aware of the treasures that await, in Boston's outer harbor—the Boston Harbor Islands.

Think for a moment of a place with more than 130 species of birds. Atlantic sunrises and Boston skyline sunsets. Merchant ships, yacht races, and lobster boats. Historic forts, lighthouses, summer cottages, and ruins from a bygone era of social programs. Sacred American Indian sites. Ferry trips, nature trails, interpretive tours, school programs, kayaking, camping, symphony concerts, and kite-flying contests. Tales of shipwrecks, pirates, and ghosts. The Boston Harbor Islands are a unique national park of thirty-four islands and coastal peninsulas managed by a partnership of government and private owners for our education and pleasure.

The glaciers of the last ice age pushed earth ahead of them, forming sandy Cape Cod as a terminal moraine. They scoured the earth below, leaving sculpted mounds of glacial till known as drumlins. As the melting glaciers receded 15,000 years ago, the ocean level rose and the only partially submerged drumlin field in what is now the United States became what we know today as the Boston Harbor Islands. These islands continue to erode. Two of them, Hangman and Sheep, will likely disappear in the twenty-first century.

BETWEEN THE WHARVES OF BOSTON
and the sea . . . are seventy-five islands
and islets, fifty notable projections . . .
and a great many shoals and reefs. . . .
The attractiveness of its harbor is to
be reckoned no insignificant element
of the prosperity of the city.

—Frederick Law Olmsted,
    to Boston City Council, 1887

Sunrise, Thompson Island and beyond

Commuter ferries, near Spectacle Island (*above*)

WE GO DOWN TO THE HARBOR WHEN THE SUN IS FIERCE
on our city homes, and breathe in the fresh coolness
of its breezes; we rejoice in the beauties of its many
islands, and restfully dream of the romances, ancient
and modern, that encircle every one.

—Julia Knowlton Dyer,
   The Islands of Boston Harbor, 1904

Approaching Graves Light with the U.S. Coast Guard (*overleaf*)

9

IN 1865 THE FORTRESS
received no less a pris-
oner than Alexander
H. Stephens, the
Vice-President of the
Confederate States, who
remained under guard
here for five months.
His fate was not severe;
for this captivity took
place in the summer and
early autumn, and was
solaced by many kind
attentions from the
gentlemen of Boston.

—M. F. Sweetser,
  King's Handbook of
  Boston Harbor, 1882

Boston Landmarks Orchestra,
Fort Warren, Georges Island

METHINKS AN ISLAND WOULD BE THE MOST DESIRABLE OF LANDED PROPERTY, for it seems like a little world by itself; and the water may answer for the atmosphere that surrounds planets. The boys swinging, two together, standing up, and almost causing the ropes and their bodies to stretch out horizontally. On our departure they ranged themselves on the rails of the fence, and, being dressed in blue, looked not unlike a flock of pigeons.

—Nathaniel Hawthorne, describing his visit to the Farm School,
  Thompson Island (in *King's Handbook of Boston Harbor*, 1882)

Wreck of barge, Green Island

Archeologists have traced human habitation of the islands back 8,000 years. A 4,100-year-old skeleton found on one island is one of the oldest discovered in New England. American Indians farmed the islands prior to the arrival of European settlers in the seventeenth century. As European settlements grew, conflicts arose, culminating in King Philip's War. During the war, colonists incarcerated about a thousand American Indians on the islands, where perhaps half of them perished during the winter of 1675–76.

The islands were a summer resort for many Bostonians beginning in the early nineteenth century, with hotels on Spectacle, Gallops, Peddocks, and Rainsford Islands. The islands' history is more influenced by the pre–Civil War belief that isolation and fresh air were beneficial for social and health problems. A quarantine hospital on Deer Island treated nearly 5,000 immigrants in its first two years during the Irish Potato Famine of the 1840s. As many as 4,000 Europeans may be buried there. A quarantine hospital on Rainsford Island was succeeded by a home for delinquent boys. The chronic care hospital on Long Island still houses certain of Boston's social service operations. Bumpkin Island was home to the Burrage Hospital for paraplegic children. The Thompson Island asylum for indigent boys evolved into an agricultural and vocational school, and is now the Thompson Island Outward Bound Education Center.

THE HISTORY OF THE PRINCIPAL ISLANDS
of Boston Harbor is in some respects
the most interesting frontier history
of the town itself.

—David McCord,
    "About Boston," 1948

Lighthouse keepers' inscriptions, Little Brewster Island

Oil shed, Lovells Island

LOVELLS ALSO HAS AN AWESOME, OLD MILITARY PARADE GROUND that you can use to play a bunch of different sports and games. We chose to play nine innings of tough whiffleball, and a little bit of football! It was so cool because there is a huge, open field with an old battle station overlooking the field and the ocean! It feels a little bit like an actual stadium—complete with a press box overlooking the field—as you smash homeruns or catch winning touchdowns!

—Odyssey School at South Boston High School,
  Adventure on the Boston Harbor Islands, Summer 2003

ALMOST EVERY BOSTON BOY LEARNED TO SWIM, pull an oar, and to sail a small spritsail-rigged boat. His education was not complete until he had gotten lost in the fog, and spent the night on an island in Boston harbor.

—Samuel Eliot Morison, *The Maritime History of Massachusetts 1783-1860*, 1921

Team-building exercise, Outward Bound program, Thompson Island

By the 1980s, Boston's harbor was considered the most polluted in the country. A state-of-the-art wastewater treatment plant, opened on Deer Island in the 1990s and serving forty-three communities, changed all that. Beaches throughout the harbor are now safe for swimming. The best sand beaches are on Spectacle, Lovells, and Gallops Islands, while rocky beaches provide a habitat for invertebrates and animals. Mussel beds and barnacles predominate in the intertidal zone. There are freshwater marshes on Long, Peddocks, and Middle Brewster, and ponds on Thompson and Worlds End. The drumlins, once forested, were cleared for subsistence farming and fortifications, and now feature mostly grass and sumac. Some islands are of exposed bedrock, including puddingstone (it looks like pudding!) and slate. Slate Island was once a quarry for its namesake.

The saltwater marshes (the most productive of all ecosystems), mud flats, and inland vegetation of the Harbor Islands support over 130 species of migratory and indigenous birds. Scientists have just discovered that the islands are the southernmost major nesting ground for eider ducks. There are rookeries for egrets, herons, gulls, and cormorants on the outer islands, and on Sarah Island. Animals include rabbits, raccoons, skunks, squirrels, and various rodents. Muskrats found their way to Spectacle Island after it was capped with landfill from Boston's "Big Dig," and they played havoc with the newly planted trees. Harbor seals visit in the winter.

Sewage digesters, Deer Island Treatment Plant

DEARE ILANDE, SO-CALLED BECAUSE OF THE DEARE
which often swimme thither from the Maine, when
they are chased by the Woolves. Some have killed
sixteen Deare in a day upon this Ilande.

—Traveler to Boston, shortly after the town was
    settled (identified by Edward Rowe Snow as
    William Wood, 1634)

ONE DAY AS BILLY MCLEOD
was strolling along the
beach he found a tiny
baby seal which he took
into the house. The seal
soon became attached to
the family, and in a few
weeks was performing
feats of unusual agility.

—Edward Rowe Snow,
   *The Islands of Boston
   Harbor,* 1935

Snowy egret, Sarah Island rookery

WE SURVEYED BIRDS DURING MAY AND JUNE ON 26 ISLANDS and one mainland park in Boston Harbor from 2001 to 2003. We detected 136 species of which 67 species were suspected of breeding. . . . We documented 73 Common Eider (*Somateria mollisma*) nests on Calf, Green, Middle Brewster, and Outer Brewster Islands in 2003, making Boston Harbor one of the largest, southernmost nesting areas on the western Atlantic Ocean.

—Peter W. C. Paton, Rebecca J. Harris, and
  Carol L. Trocki, Boston Harbor Islands Science
  Symposium, 2003

Calf Island

IT'S A PLACE EVERY CHILD
should visit to understand
our cultural history, our
natural history, and our
place in the world.

—Katherine F. Abbott,
   Commissioner of the
   Department of
   Conservation and
   Recreation, 2004

Nest of common eider, Green Island

IN 1725 . . . SO MANY BEARS WERE BEING KILLED AROUND BOSTON
that some of the beasts took to the ocean for refuge, several of
them swimming across to Spectacle Island.

—Edward Rowe Snow, *The Islands of Boston Harbor*, 1935

Botanist Ted Elliman on Spectacle Island (*left*)

"The Graves" (*overleaf*)

IN 2001 AND 2002, 32 ISLANDS in Boston Harbor were surveyed and inventoried for vascular plant species. To date, 509 species in 99 plant families have been identified on these islands. A total of 234 species (46%) are exotic plants. On many islands, non-native plants account for 50% or more of the total flora.

—Ted Elliman,
    Boston Harbor Islands
    Science Symposium, 2003

Marsh grass glasswort, Snake Island

Nineteenth-century sewage treatment facility, Moon Island, with new facility visible in the distance

IN THE END, WE CONSERVE ONLY WHAT WE LOVE. We will love only what we understand. We will understand only what we are taught.

—Baba Dioum, Senegalese conservationist

*F*ortifications have protected Boston's natural harbor since colonial times. Gun emplacements, bunkers and barracks abound on the islands. Fort Warren, a National Historic Landmark on Georges Island, served as a harbor fortification and prison from the Civil War through World War II. It is a marvelous star-shaped fort in excellent condition. On Peddocks Island there are twenty-six buildings remaining from Fort Andrews, mostly abandoned for fifty years. They constitute a rare example of a 1900 Endicott Period coastal fort. Seawalls in various states of disrepair border numerous islands.

Institutional ruins from hospitals, prisons, and reform schools remind us of the earlier "out-of-sight, out-of-mind" doctrine. These structures were built to last, but most did not. An exception is Outward Bound's handsome campus of Georgian school buildings on Thompson Island. The prominent chimney on Calf Island, a navigational landmark, is all that remains of Benjamin Cheney's 1902 summer retreat. The thirty wood-framed cottages on Peddocks Island, originally a fishing community, include the last occupied summer residences. The Boston fire and police departments have training facilities on Moon Island.

Boston Light, on Little Brewster, is also a National Historic Landmark. Built in 1716, it is the nation's oldest light station, and is currently its last U.S. Coast Guard–staffed lighthouse. Graves Light and Long Island Head Light are listed on the National Register of Historic Places.

TO ONE WHO THOROUGHLY EXPLORES THE ISLAND, there will recur vivid reminiscences of the mysterious castles of romance and history. He will find here a sally-port, a postern, a draw-bridge, and a portcullis. Here, too, are passages underground and in the walls; turret staircases, huge vaulted apartments, and safe and dark dungeons. . . . It only needs a dark and windy night to make almost real the description of the Castle of Udolpho, with its clanging sounds of chains, its sweeping gusts of air, its strange moanings and howlings, and the startling noise of some sudden clang of a shutting door reverberating through the arches.

—Col. F. J. Parker, "Thirty-Second Regiment,"
   in *King's Handbook of Boston Harbor*, 1882

Interior of Fort Warren, Georges Island

IN YEARS NOT LONG PAST, SOMETIMES, OF A PLEASANT SUMMER SUNDAY, scores of boats, dories, and yachts would make a rush from the city to this sequestered spot, and their crews would congregate in a dense circular crowd on the greensward. From the general scattering apparent if the harbor-police boat approached, it was evident that these summer-tourists were not on the best terms with the law; and the general belief is, that the art of pugilism had here a favored shrine.

—*King's Handbook of Boston Harbor,* 1882

Outward Bound campus, Thompson Island (*previous*)

Ruins of 1902 summer mansion, Calf Island (*right*)

SINCE IT IS A DRUMLIN-FORMED ISLAND WITH LONG STRETCHES OF BEACH,
Great Brewster offers easy access to the surrounding intertidal zone.
In contrast, the island's rocky shoreline in the northwest part is dotted
with a number of small tidal pools—micromarine environments cre-
ated by the ebbing tide leaving behind pockets of water in crevices,
grooves and low areas.

—Emily and David Kales, *All About the Boston Harbor Islands*, 1993

Boston Light, viewed from Great Brewster Island

Outer harbor sunrise from Boston Light lantern, Little Brewster Island

THANKS AND BEST WISHES TO THE LIGHTHOUSE KEEPER OF BOSTON LIGHT for his well and bright kept light and great lookout and especially for ringing the bell on my approaching the light on 6 December [1862] at 2 [o'clock] in the snowstorm that was raging at the time. By ringing the bell enabled me to judge my distance better and by it gained the Harbor.

Very Respectfully Yours,
Franklin Shute Master
Brig Isaac Carver
of Searsport, Maine

—Cited in Snowman and Thomson, *Boston Light: A Historical Perspective*, 1999

THE LIGHT-HOUSE WAS BUILT IN 1819, AND IS A ROUND IRON TOWER, attached to a neat little house, which serves the keeper as a home. On two sides it is surrounded by ramparts, which rest upon the very edges of the steep cliff, and, though at present of little service as defence, yet certainly are picturesque, being clad with verdure, and dotted all over with daisies and buttercups, forming by their great mounds and embrasures just the most delightful place in the world for a merry game of hide-and-seek. It is pleasant to sit there, and look off across the Bay, beyond all land, until the purple sea is lost in the purple sky, watching the tiny yachts and great ships coming in and going out, and the flag-decked steamers, from whose decks distant music floats upward.

—M. F. Sweetser, *King's Handbook of Boston Harbor*, 1882

Long Island Head Light

MASSACHUSETTS BAY IN SAILING-SHIP DAYS WAS DANGEROUS WATER in dirty weather. Its irregular bottom gives the lead-line no clue. When a northeast snowstorm obscured Boston Light, a mistake of a quarter-point fetched up many a good ship on Cohasset rocks or the Graves.

—Samuel Eliot Morison,
   Maritime History of Massachusetts, 1921

The U.S. Congress added the Boston Harbor Islands to the national park system in 1996. This unit is unique in that the National Park Service controls none of the 1,600 acres of this national park area. The thirty-four islands and peninsulas are owned and maintained by a group of federal, state, city and private/nonprofit entities. Congress's enabling legislation required that a partnership of these "owners" be formed to develop and implement a general management plan that would "protect the islands as a resource of national significance and make the island system an integral part of the life of the surrounding communities and region, while improving public knowledge and access for education, recreation, and tranquility within an urban area." The thirteen-member Partnership is supported by a twenty-eight-member Advisory

Council representing seven public interest groups. A National Park Service office oversees integration of the park as a unit of the national system. In an unusual arrangement for a national park, federal support is limited by law to no more than one quarter of the funds needed to develop the Boston Harbor Islands park. The remainder is provided by the state, municipal, and nonprofit Partners, as well as the private sector through the Island Alliance.

Over the last several years a team of scientists has taken inventory of the vast physical and natural resources of the park. This knowledge base is guiding the Partnership in responsibly developing certain islands for more intense visitation and public programming, while protecting and managing the sensitive resources on other islands.

NEARBY THESE GRAY ROCKS

Enclos'd in a box

Lies Hatter Cox

Who died of smallpox.

—Epitaph on rock near

1832 fever hospital on

Rainsford Island (cited

in Snow, *The Islands of*

Boston Harbor, 1935)

Richard Bell, intertidal zone scientist, Little Calf Island (*previous*)

Volunteers cleaning up Rainsford Island (*above*)

Scott LaGreca, taking lichen inventory, Middle Brewster Island

TO THE CASUAL VISITOR, THE BOSTON HARBOR ISLANDS provide an interesting excursion; to the archaeologist, however, they are a working laboratory for uncovering the past. In fact, although many of the archaeological sites on the islands have been destroyed over the centuries by human settlement and by erosion, experts consider the Boston Harbor Islands (along with the adjacent river basins) to be the single most important area for understanding the early history of this part of the New England coast.

—Barbara Luedtke, cited in Kales and Kales,
   All About the Boston Harbor Islands, 1993

THE EDUCATIONAL AND RECREATIONAL
opportunities on the islands are
tremendous, and when people are
better educated about the environ-
ment, everybody benefits.

—Richard F. Delaney,
  cited in *Boston Globe*, 1996

Boston, from University of Massachusetts research vessel

The Boston Harbor Islands national park area is open year-round, but ferry service is seasonal from spring through fall. There are special boat tours even in the winter. Most island visitors depart by ferry from Long Wharf on the Boston waterfront, itself a National Historic Landmark, and one of several mainland gateways. The trip out is exhilarating with the salt air, views back at the Boston skyline, commercial boat traffic, sea birds, and a release from the tensions of urban life. The mainland ferry drops many passengers off at Georges Island. Here they can take guided tours of historic Fort Warren (another National Historic Landmark) and learn about ghosts and prison escapes; they can picnic; and they can enjoy special events such as outdoor concerts and athletic contests. From Georges Island visitors can take shuttle ferries to a number of the other islands and experience the unique walking trails, natural beauty and historic structures on each. Permits are available for camping on a number of the islands. Spectacle Island is a "new" island, now that the horse-rendering plant and refuse dump have been capped with fill from Boston's "Big Dig." Docks and trails are fully handicapped-accessible, and the island is a demonstration project for sustainable design. Schools use the islands as outdoor laboratories for planned curricula. And the Thompson Island Outward Bound Education Center has its own outdoor learning programs for inner-city youth and visitors. An eco-retreat is planned as an adaptive use project at Fort Andrews on Peddocks Island.

Ferries are not a requirement for visiting the park. Deer Island and Worlds End (a Frederick Law Olmsted design), for instance, are connected to the mainland and have extensive trail systems. Private boats and kayaks afford access to most islands, but landing is discouraged on some, particularly those with bird rookeries or unprotected ruins.

Edward Rowe Snow, docking at Bumpkin Island

AND IT IS AN INTERESTING BIOLOGICAL FACT
that all of us have in our veins the exact
same percentages of salt in our blood, in our
sweat, in our tears. We are tied to the ocean.
And when we go back to the sea—whether
it is to sail or to watch it—we are going
back from where we came.

—President John F. Kennedy, 1962

ONCE THE ISLANDS WERE BODIES OF FOLIAGE.
Seen one against another and grouping
with woody headlands, they formed
scenery of grace and amenity, cheerful,
genial, and hospitable. But long ago they
were despoiled for petty private gains, and
the harbor made artificially bald, raw,
bleak, prosaic, inhospitable.

—Frederick Law Olmsted, 1886

Path to nature preserve, Peddocks Island

THE BOSTON HARBOR ISLANDS ARE THIS CITY'S SHINING GEMS, providing recreation, enjoyment and new opportunities for residents and visitors alike. Each of the harbor's thirty-four islands has its own distinctive history and identity, and each has a unique role to play in the exciting future of our city.

—Craig P. Coy, Chief Executive Officer, Massachusetts Port Authority, 2004

Cross-country ski tracks, Deer Island

If you have not yet visited the Boston Harbor Islands, you are in for a surprise. If you have visited but once, you are tempted to return. If you have explored a number of the islands, you are fortunate to have begun peeling away the cloak of secrecy and reveal the sensory layers of nature and history that inhabit these islands.

No two trips into this national park are alike. Weather and sea conditions are constantly changing. You may be sharing discoveries with family and friends, or you may be reveling in the contemplative solitude attainable right in the front yard of one of the country's great metropolitan areas. When you step back on the mainland, you realize you have just completed an experience that will not be duplicated. This is what draws us back, and back again. What new birds will we see? What was it like for Native Americans to live out here in the summers and harvest the bounty of the islands? How did immigrants cope with disease and death in the quarantine stations? Who were the master builders of Fort Warren? Who were the social workers who inscribed their tours of duty on the rocks? How will the Boston skyline look in another twenty years?

  The Boston Harbor Islands are waiting. Bring your camera.

Great black-backed gull, Middle Brewster Island

CONSIDER WHAT THIS HARBOR AND ITS ISLANDS HAVE SEEN: in our own time, grand parades of tall ships to celebrate our city's seafaring heritage; a hundred years ago, shiploads of immigrants arriving to start a new life; before that, ships bearing British tea that would stain the harbor and start a rebellion; and at the very beginning a small band of colonists who dreamed, as John Winthrop said in 1630 and John Kennedy echoed in 1960, "of a city upon a hill."

—Historian and author William Martin, 2004

EVERY SUNRISE IN NEW ENGLAND
is more full of wonder than the
Pyramids, every sunset more
magnificent than the Transfigu-
ration. Why go to see the Bay
of Naples when we have not
yet seen Boston Harbor?

—James Freeman Clarke,
   in *King's Handbook*
   of Boston Harbor, 1882

Sunset from lantern of Boston Light, Little Brewster Island

ACKNOWLEDGMENTS

I AM INDEBTED TO MANY WHO SHARE A PASSION FOR THE BOSTON HARBOR Islands and who have helped make this book possible. Park superintendent George Price enabled me to accompany researchers to the less accessible islands, and Bruce Jacobson ensured my text passed factual muster. Sally Snowman, keeper of Boston Light, inspired me with her own book, *Boston Light: A Historical Perspective*. I have new friends among the scientists and organizers of the natural resources survey, and Russ Bowles made sure I returned safely from many islands on the versatile UMass landing craft. Support for turning my photography project into a book has come from DCR Commissioner Kathy Abbott, Doug Welch at the Island Alliance, Jeff Redmond and numerous knowledgeable alumni of New Directions, historian Robert J. Allison, my Advisory Council partner Greg Ketchen, and my brother-in-law, the author Peter Decker. Many proposed quotations or wrote short statements, including Alice Boelter, Marianne Connolly, Craig Coy, Ted Elliman, Sean Hennessey, David Kales, Tom Lindberg, Larry Lowenthal, Barbara Mackey, William Martin, and staff at the USS Constitution Museum.

We wouldn't have a book without the expertise and enthusiasm of Commonwealth Editions. Publisher Webster Bull became a BHI convert. He edited my text and, with series editor Andrew Borsari, the photographs as well. Penny Stratton, Russell Scahill, and Anne Rolland worked to bring it all together as a finished product, with design and layout by Peter Blaiwas and Benjamin Jenness of Vern Associates, Inc.

SHERMAN "PAT" MORSS is an architect specializing in preservation projects, including New York Harbor's Ellis Island. A member of the Advisory Council of the Boston Harbor Islands National Recreation Area, he has been photographing the islands for the past five years. A native of Boston's North Shore and a graduate of the University of Pennsylvania, he now lives with his wife, Anne-Lise, in Gloucester, Massachusetts.

Photo by Anne-Lise Morss

NOTE FROM THE AUTHOR

When appointed to the park's Advisory Council, I had to admit that, although familiar with Boston Harbor, I had actually set foot only on Georges Island. Clearly I had to become more familiar with the island resources if I were to effectively promote the park. Photography became my means for doing just that. Not only did I come to understand the marvelous natural and cultural diversity of these islands, but I also came to know many of their devoted advocates. The new Partnership of island "owners" is in the process of creating a national treasure that is greater than the sum of its parts. This effort will succeed through increased visitorship and public participation in recreational and educational programs. My hope is that this book will increase such interest in the Boston Harbor Islands.

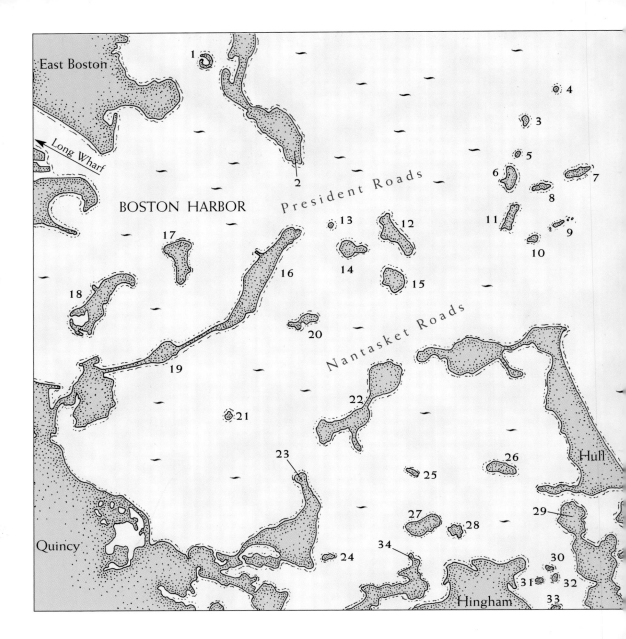

East Boston

1

Long Wharf

2

BOSTON HARBOR

President Roads

4

3

5

6

7

8

11

9

10

13

12

17

14

15

16

Nantasket Roads

18

20

19

22

21

Hull

23

26

25

29

Quincy

27

28

24

34

30

31

32

33

Hingham